HARLEY-DAVIDSON
the cult lives on

HARLEY-DAVIDSON
the cult lives on

Gerald Foster

Osprey Colour Series

Published in 1984 by Osprey Publishing Limited,
12–14 Long Acre, London WC2E 9LP
Member company of the George Philip Group

British Library Cataloguing in Publication Data

Foster, Gerald
   Cult of the Harley-Davidson 2.—(Osprey colour series)
   1. Harley-Davidson motorcycle
   I. Title
   629.2′275   TL448.H3

ISBN 0-85045-577-4

Editor Tim Parker
Design Joy FitzSimmons

Filmset by Tameside Filmsetting Limited,
Ashton-under-Lyne, Lancashire
Printed in Hong Kong

You don't just show up on a Harley. You ARRIVE. – David K. Wright, author of *The Harley-Davidson Motor Company, An Official Eighty Year History.*

Bespectacled old lady serving breakfast to a mountain of a biker in the Sturgis senior citizen center. – 'Would you like some more coffee, sonny?'

Bridesmaid to her beau at a wedding where everyone rode to the reception on their Harley-Davidsons. – 'There better not be any fuckin' Armor All on that seat, Charlie! I don't want this dress ruined.'

'How did we tattoo the pigs, man? Shit, it was easy! We just fed 'em on rye bread soaked in beer until they couldn't stand up no more. They didn't feel a thing believe me but boy did they have hangovers next morning. Had a terrible time strapping 'em onto the hood of the Chevy for the trip here. I guess they had the last laugh though 'cause the air conditioner gave out right after we left home; the little fuckers were cooler than we were. How far? Oh, I guess Oklahoma City to Sturgis is about 800 miles or so. Did folk stare at us? Yeah, I guess some of them did now I come to think of it. Perhaps they had never seen tattooed hogs before.'

The Harley-Davidson cult is special. Nothing more needs to be said. Just enjoy the next few pages.

5

We are receiving your mail and we love it!

Apparently Gerald Foster started something with *Cult of the Harley-Davidson* we didn't anticipate – your sending in photographs and suggestions of the ways in which the world's best loved motorcycle affects and invades your everyday life. Please keep those letters coming to our London, England address, marked for Gerald Foster, and we'll make sure he gets them. In the meantime, watch for the next 'Cult' book; you may be part of it.

Thanks must go to Don Edmunds, Gordon and Gary Schroeder, Bill Hoeker, Hawkeye and Shawnee, Debbie (you're incredible) and JR, Frank and Kathy Bailor, Psycho Ward – a man who cares about those less fortunate than himself, Bud Ekins for access to the best collection of antique motorcycles in the world, and the people of Sturgis, South Dakota, USA.

This book is dedicated to the people the world over who live, love and ride Harley-Davidson motorcycles.

Contents

Sturgis is . . .	8
Biker art and jewelry	30
Battle of the Twins	44
Skin art	54
Harley people are characters	66
More bikes and trikes	78
Tee shirt mania	92
Military and antique	102
Evolution	120
Overcoming	126

8

Sturgis is ...

Left A normal morning in the farming community of Sturgis, South Dakota

Below The meeting place and headquarters of the annual Black Hills Classic Motorcycle Rally, an event which has endured with only two time outs (for a world war) since 1938

Estimates of the number of motorcyclists who descend upon Sturgis range from a conservative 10,000 to 60,000 and up. As many spend their time touring the Black Hills an accurate count is virtually impossible

13

Below left Pins in a map of the world at rally headquarters show bikers present from every state in the union, plus Canada and Mexico. In addition Northern Europe, South Africa, Japan, Australia, and New Zealand were represented

Centre . . . selling things

Below The Black Hills Classic could very easily be renamed the Black Hills Classic Harley-Davidson Rally since ninety-nine percent of all bikes present were Harleys

. . . tattooing things

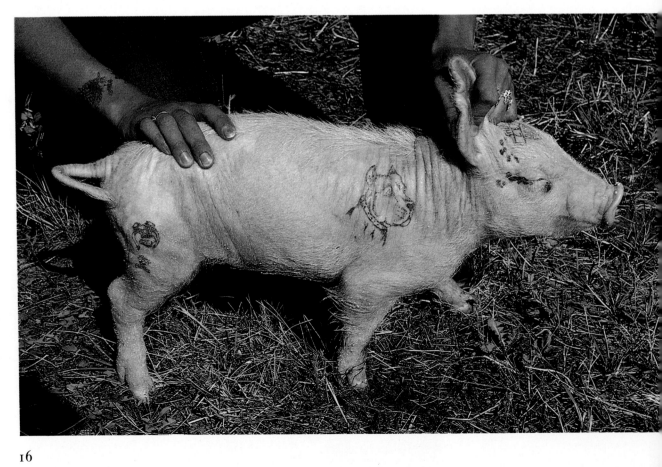

Right . . . watching for the many police watching for open beer containers on the street

Below . . . painting things

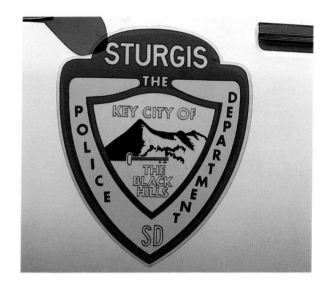

Left . . . watching the world go by on Main Street; without doubt one of the more pleasant pastimes of Sturgis week

Below . . . looking out

. . . an all you can eat breakfast prepared and
served by the town's senior citizens

Right . . . warm days

Below . . . automobile drivers not seeing bikes. Luckily no one was hurt

. . . a place to cool off

. . . legal engines for sale

. . . somewhere to eat

. . . a place to sell your bike

. . . a car wash called 'Splash and Dash'?

. . . above all else Harleys of all kinds

. . . the people who ride them

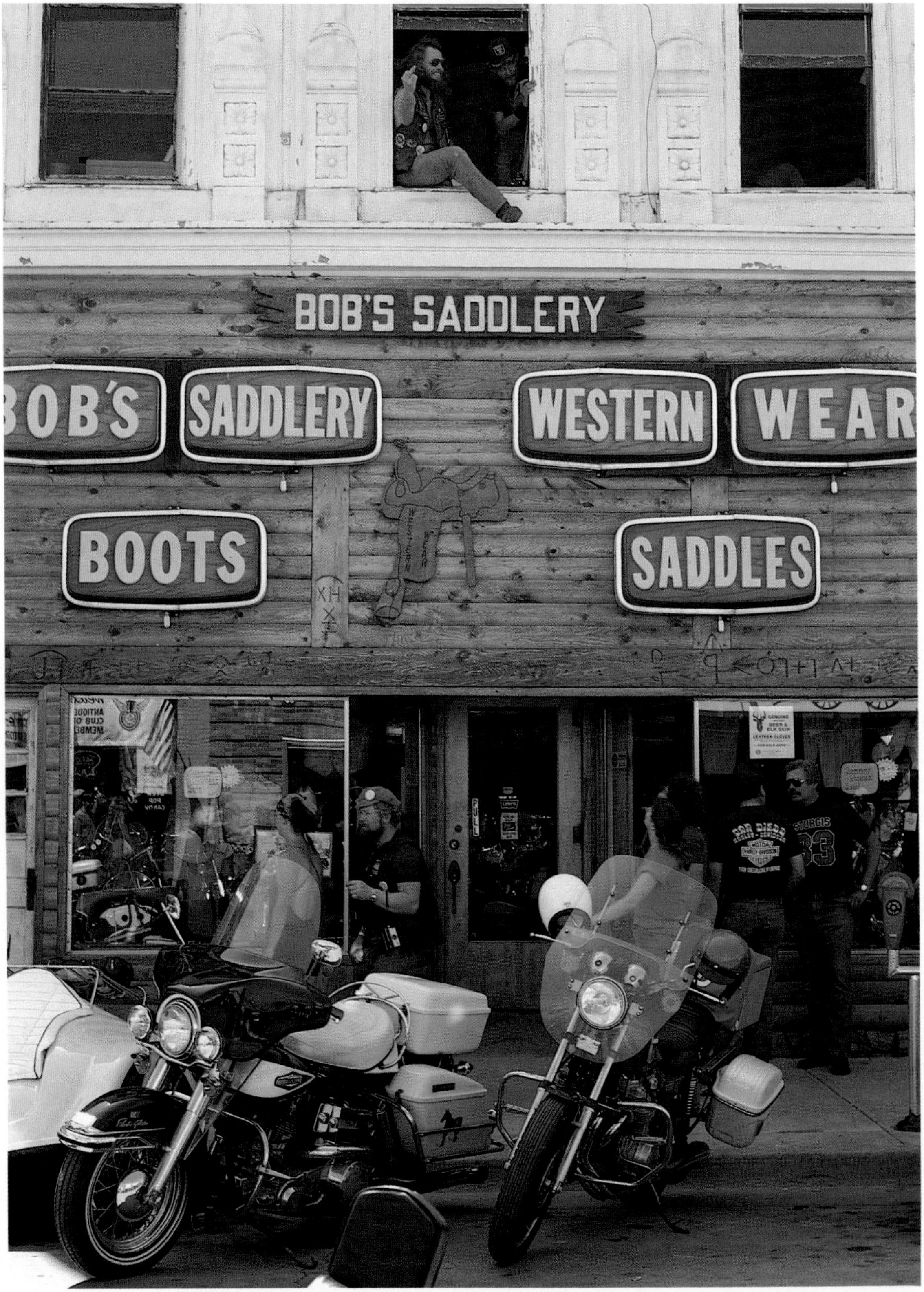
BOB'S SADDLERY
BOB'S
SADDLERY
WESTERN
WEAR
BOOTS
SADDLES

Above . . . a visit to Mount Rushmore

Left . . . and good old fashioned fun

Right . . . a tall friend to watch over your bike

Biker art and jewelry

Left Miniature pewter engine under glass. A steal at seventy dollars

Below A little overdressed perhaps?

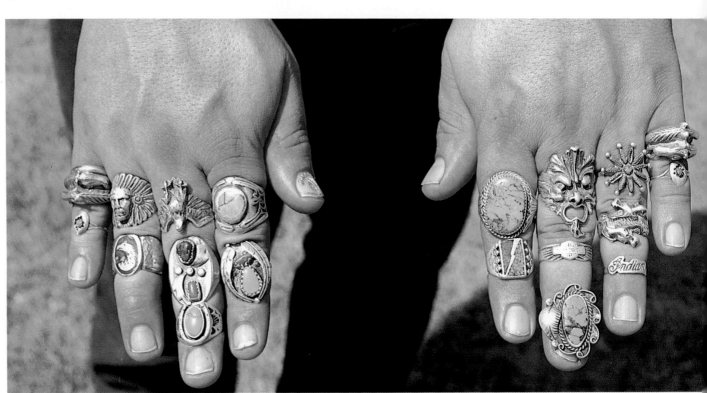

Can designer engineer boots be far behind?

It's still a Harley

Battle of the Twins

Left and below To the delight of the fans Harley-Davidsons are being raced on the pavement once more. This time around it's Battle of the Twins, and XR1000s in various classes are proving formidable competition for the Ducatis, Guzzis, BMWs, Triumphs, and all

Big Dell'Orto carburettors suck in lots of air.
Rider's knee can get in the way

Gene Church – expert modified and overall
winner at Laguna Seca, 1983

The pits, Laguna Seca

49

Left Variety is the spice of life. The amateur modified class on the line at Laguna Seca

Gene Church awaiting the start – all appears calm – Laguna Seca, 1983

XR1000s are also appearing at your local drag
strip

Skin art

'Harley-Davidson has to be the only revered corporate identity in the world. I mean, when did you ever see the name Ford, or Alcoa, or Bell Telephone tattooed on someone's body.'
A biker

We complain when pictures of our tattoos give no credit to the artist; I suppose we should sign our work like painters do.
A tatooist

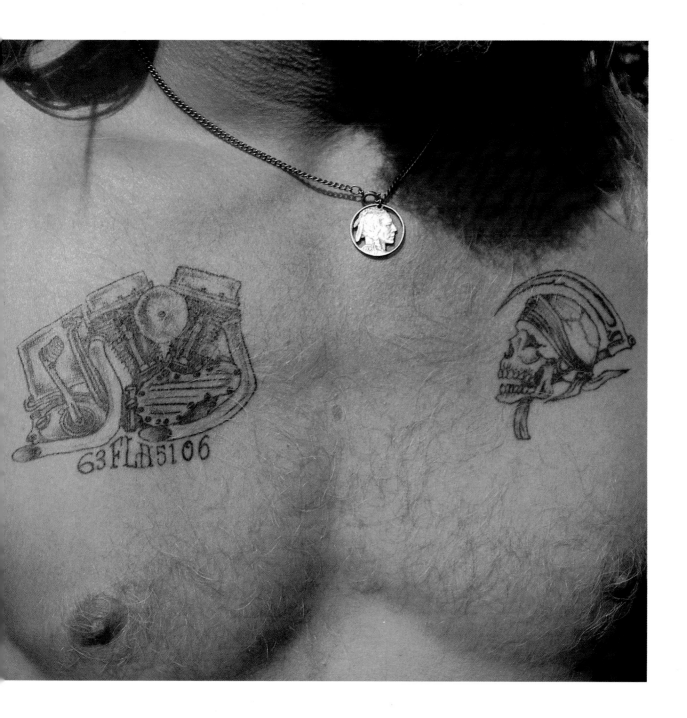

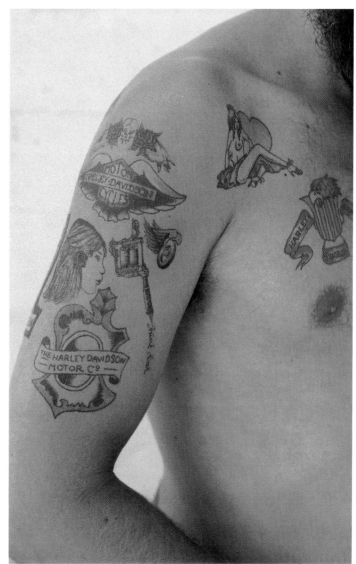

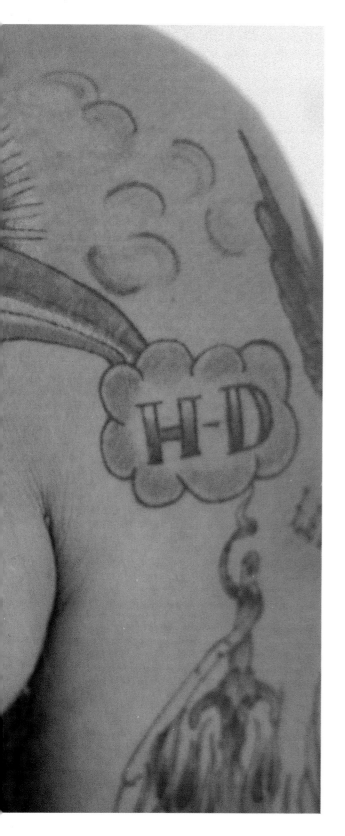

63

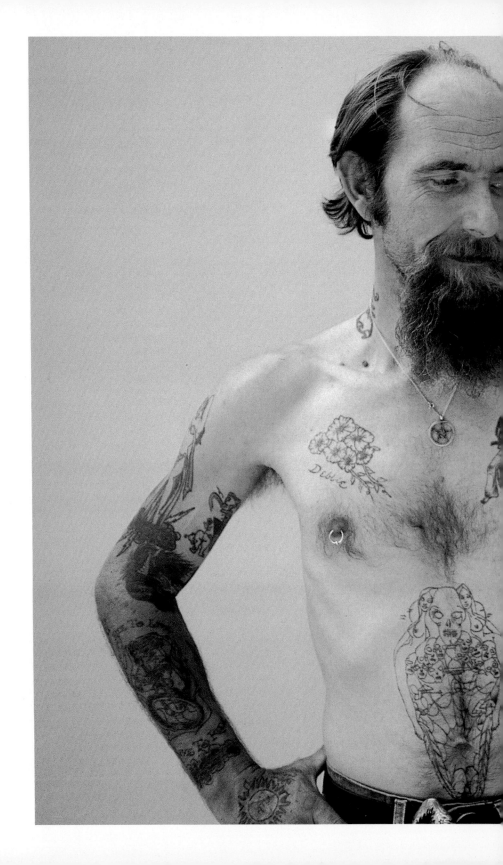

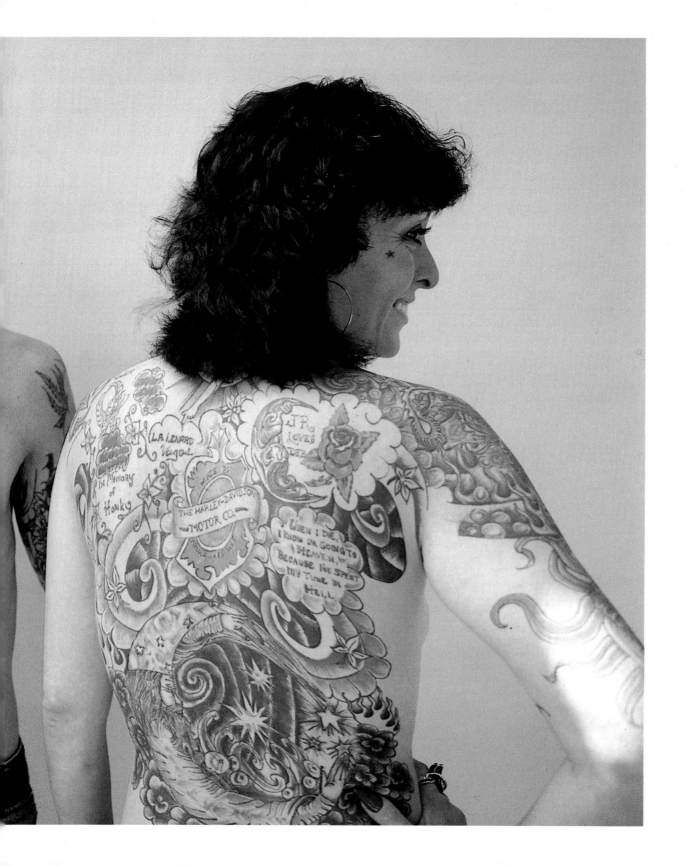

Harley people are characters

Far left You have to admire a man with a sense of humor

Left Rolling into Sturgis in an old ex-church bus which now forms the basis of his travelling 'Cycle Emporium', owner Buddha 'T' was heard to tell someone, 'Yeah, belonging to a church for so long she's got a lot of good karma in her.' See overleaf

Right Most people are happy with a cat or a
dog

Below left 'You've got a broken leg and less than two dollars in your pocket, yet you smile when some bozo wants to take your picture!'

Right Another Harley couple at Sturgis –
Arlen Ness bike

Below You should see him when he really
gets upset!

Categorizing people is something we all do usually with only limited success. Take Gordon Martin, attorney-at-law, for example. Without the motorcycle would you have guessed he was a longtime Harley-Davidson owner and enthusiast? Which only goes to show you can't judge someone who rides a Harley by the clothes he does or doesn't wear. Enjoy your new bike, Gordon

. . . the Ol' Lady getting more ticked off by
the minute when the scoot doesn't start

More bikes and trikes

Perfect K

Left Someone, somewhere is always wanting to build a chopper or customise a Harley. Bob Bell and Santee Industries probably manufacture and sell more custom frames for Harley-Davidsons than anyone except Harley-Davidson

Below Show job

Blow job

Trike with boat deck

Overleaf Salt tracker

Left Colorful 45
Below . . . a mother of a tire

. . . a foxy looking lady without a chaise

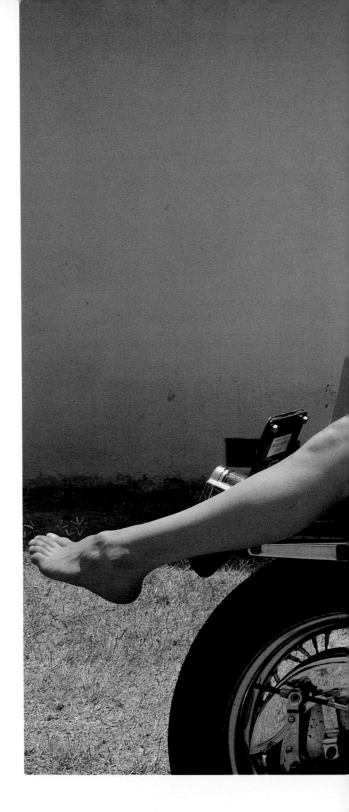

Harley "45"

HARLEY DAVIDSON
GENUINE
WORLD'S
NO.1
BRAND
QUALITY
Milwaukee
IRON
MOTORCYCLES
100 PROOF
MADE BY AMERICANS
FOR AMERICANS
EST 1903

MADE IN MILWAUKEE

BY THE PEOPLE FOR THE PEOPLE

IF THEY WON'T ALLOW
HARLEYS
IN HEAVEN
WE'LL RIDE THEM
STRAIGHT TO
HELL

OUT
WA
ALL O

HARLEY PRAYER

FASTER SCOOTERS
LOOSER WOMEN
OLDER WHISKEY

Harley
honey

MUSTACHE
RIDES
25¢

PARTY TILL YOU PUKE
DRINK TILL YOU STINK
SMOKE TILL YOU CHOKE
AND GET TO HELL OUT

I'M HIS
BECAUSE HE RIDES A
HARLEY

JAPANESE
MOTORCYCLE

REPAIR KIT

My Daddy
Rides A Harley

U.S. FOOD & DRUG
ADMINISTRATION
COCAINE
RESEARCH DEPT.

HARLEY DAVIDSON
MADE IN
EST USA 1903

HARLI

Tee shirt mania

Left Dirty washing
Below Young at heart

94

Left Even a sunburnt nose cannot detract

Below A new California law permits relatives of a victim to make recommendations regarding punishment to a judge during the sentencing phase of a trial

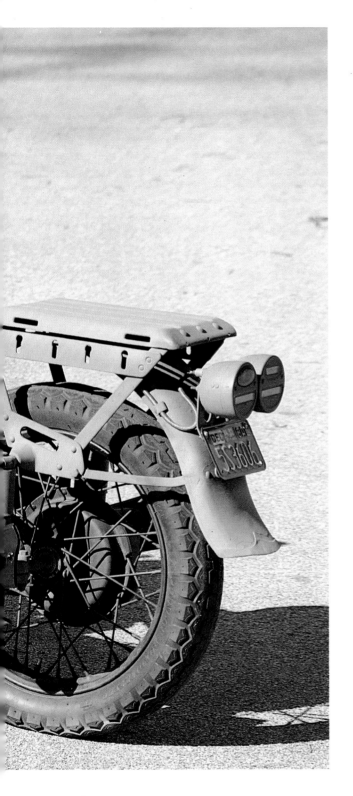

Military and antique

Left A somewhat rare, well restored XA military machine minus its field equipment. Patterned after a certain German manufacturer's horizontally opposed twin, the XA was a result of government involvement in the design process. Only one thousand machines were ordered and built compared to the almost ninety thousand WLA model manufactured

Below Will there ever be an XA tee shirt?

Far left Blackout lighting atop the more normal headlight

Left While the parts manual indicates a shock absorber very few were ever used due to problems of fit with the rifle scabbard

Far left The name Harley-Davidson appears only on this plate

Left 45 cu. in. opposed twin cylinder engine

Mid-twenties Big Twin and sidecar

Below 1915 was the first year a three speed
transmission was available on the twin

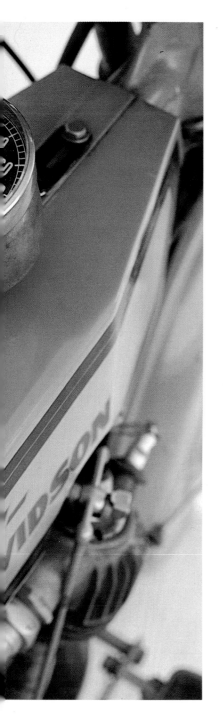

Even after a long storage this 1923 JD still
manages to exude an air of dignity

All Though many parts have been lost or rotted away and others need lots of work, this JD will eventually look better than the day it left the factory

The Sport model manufactured from 1919 thru 1922 featured a transmission mounted atop its 37 cu. in. opposed front to rear two cylinder engine

1933 alcohol burning 750 cc production hillclimber

Below Knucklehead, Panhead, Shovel-head, . . . ?
Centre Refinement *Right* FLH Special Edition

Evolution

Left In only a matter of weeks after introduction of the FXST Softail, aftermarket manufacturers were producing and selling parts and accessories to change the look of the machine. These wheels for example cost in the region of $750 a pair

Below Concealed suspension beneath the Softail engine provides the hardtail look of the fifties without the hard ride

XLX-61. A no frills Sportster

Overcoming

Below Although born with cerebral palsy Larry Walukiewicz wanted to ride a motorcycle – preferably a Harley-Davidson. A Servi-car proved to be the perfect machine. 'Please stress my ability, not my disability' he asked. Don't really see the need to Larry, you're doing a pretty good job of it yourself!

Right Mike Moody on the other hand has tackled spinal atrophy, a paralysing disease which put him a wheelchair at nineteen, in a slightly more offbeat yet no less courageous way – with a three wheeled customised electric chair. Capable of hitting eighteen miles an hour the chair is constantly being modified and upgraded to Mike's specifications. And, being in a wheelchair has not robbed Mike of his sense of humor; he is the founder of a club for wheelchair bound motorcyclists called 'Satan's Gimps'

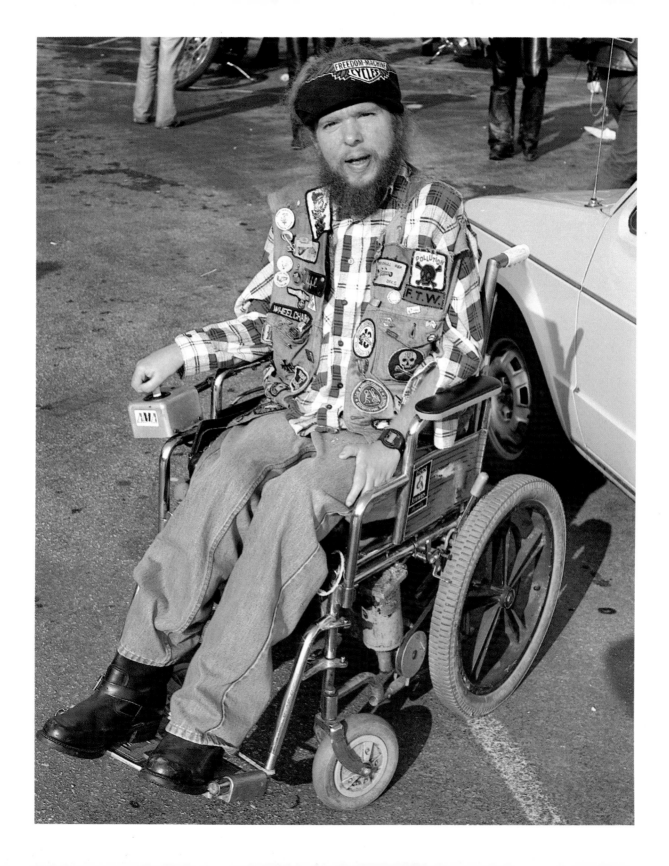

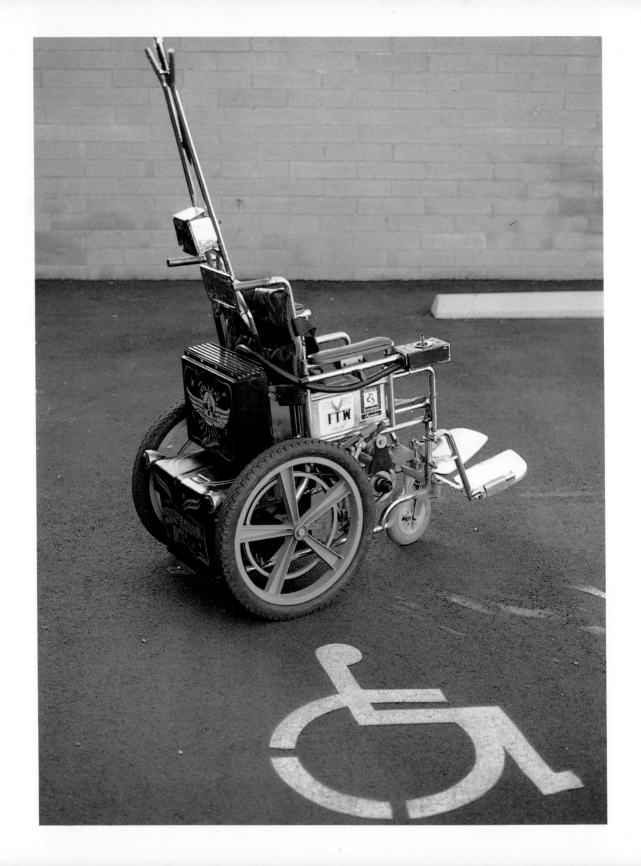